T0208487

DON'T BE
AFRAID OF YOUR
JOURNEY

DON'T BE
AFRAID OF YOUR
JOURNEY

Cynthia Marshall

DON'T BE AFRAID OF YOUR JOURNEY

iUniverse books may be ordered through booksellers or by contacting:

iUniverse
1663 Liberty Drive
Bloomington, IN 47403
www.iuniverse.com
1-800-Authors (1-800-288-4677)

Because of the dynamic nature of the Internet, any web addresses or
links contained in this book may have changed since publication and
may no longer be valid. The views expressed in this work are solely those
of the author and do not necessarily reflect the views of the publisher,
and the publisher hereby disclaims any responsibility for them.

Any people depicted in stock imagery provided by Getty Images are
models, and such images are being used for illustrative purposes only.
Certain stock imagery © Getty Images.

Scripture quotations marked KJV are from the Holy Bible, King James Version
(Authorized Version). First published in 1611. Quoted from the KJV Classic
Reference Bible, Copyright © 1983 by The Zondervan Corporation.

Scripture quotations marked NIV are taken from the Holy Bible, New
International Version®. NIV®. Copyright © 1973, 1978, 1984 by International
Bible Society. Used by permission of Zondervan. All rights reserved. [Biblica]

ISBN: 978-1-6632-0017-4 (sc)
ISBN: 978-1-6632-0018-1 (e)

Print information available on the last page.

iUniverse rev. date: 05/11/2020

Yes I'm writing. But where do I begin and what do I talk about. Am I writing something that I want to share with the world? Maybe I should just write about what everyone wants to hear.

I decided to write about what's important to me and what makes me happy. My story is important to me, my children are important, my struggles, my disappointments, and my journey. O yes and lets not forget the main important key to my life, god. He gives me the strength everyday and guides my steps. Especially when I can't see what's next, he has a way of showing me through prayer and how to get through it.

My insecurities are important to me, the lessons I learned in life, and being successful is definitely something I crave.

I am ME, CYNTHIA MARSHALL. We as women are sometimes not aware that every little part of us no matter what it is, is important. Every little thing that's important to me is apart of me.

I am valuable, I am strong, I am bold, I am beautiful, I am everything that god made me.

My journey is what made me the women I am today.

PSALMS 139:14(NIV)

"I PRAISE YOU

BECAUSE I AM

FEARFULLY AND

WONDERFULLY MADE"

I appreciate every flaw every attitude that makes me ME.. I'm the bomb.

I can remember one of the biggest mountains I had to get past was the struggle of anxiety.

I struggled with having anxiety attacks everyday that lead me to an uneasy place in life. I felt like I couldn't function.

I changed my diets, I worked out, and I started reading more, but nothing worked. I realized that it was something deeper that was affecting me.

Maybe it was my abusive marriage?

For a while my body couldn't handle any form of stress. Even at work. Answering the phone would break me down. I didn't know how to cope with it.

I would pray everyday asking god where is it coming from and how can I stop it. It was starting to take over my daily activities. Inside I was dealing with so much. I didn't know how to handle it all at once. I BEGAN TO FEEL ALONE. I felt that no one would understand the pain I was dealing with on a daily basis.

I started to become depressed because I couldn't figure it out on my own.

I started praying asking god for guidance on how to cope with this thing, this horrible thing that just couldn't allow me to get through a normal day.

Psalms 46:5 (NIV)

"God is within her,

she will not fall"

The more physical abuse I would take on the more anxiety attacks I would have.

How come I couldn't see what the issue was that was breaking me down? I couldn't see it because I was constantly blaming myself.

I was blaming myself for every time or every abusive interaction. How can I correct this or fix what has happened? Instead of me paying attention on what shouldn't be happening to me in the first place. I was focused on fixing it. But we all know that there are just somethings we cant fix. But of course us as women get so focused on our careers and taking care of home we forget or ignore the obvious.

I began to lose Cynthia.

"DON'T LET ANY
SITUATION
ALLOW YOU TO
COMPLETELY LOSE
YOURSELF. THERE
IS ONLY ONE YOU"
-CYNTHIA MARSHALL

Yes, I had money, a closet full of clothes and could buy what ever I wanted, but I had no peace. And money cant buy that. I started accepting this treatment and it became the norm.

You ask yourself now how could I allow this to become a part my life?

I started to loose what's important to me. I started to loose my insight on life. How can I make things better? That's all I kept asking myself, or who do I talk to, or who would understand. I barely understood everything myself.

But one thing I did not lose and gained more of was my personal relationship with god. I found myself talking to him more and more through out the day to the point where I just knew he was around and listening.

He's the reason I haven't lost my mind. But I still didn't understand. And I didn't realize it until I left the situation and suddenly my anxiety stopped.

It was clearly deaper. It was my overall situation. I was blinded by this not realizing my worth.

But enough about me. Because I can talk about me all day. Or do you want to hear more........

Well I have more.

Sometimes you have to lose everything and start fresh to get exactly what god wants you to have and to see. And that is yourself. God kept me, protected me, and spared me. I finally had Cynthia Marshall.

Without the all the material things I was surrounded by before that I lost, and all the negative distractions that were trying to hurt me, this is how I was able to clearly see god move, restore, and bless me in my life. I said to myself who am I now. Im still the same with or without it all.

And god helped me see that. He helped me to see that you are who I created and there is only one you. I started asking god what is my purpose through all this.

Luke 1:45 (NIV)

"Blessed is she

who

believed that the

lord would

fulfill his promises

to her"

But what's important to me now? Getting to know me the real Cynthia was finally important.

Starting over was not easy. I was 6 months pregnant with a 4 year old son at the time I left my unhealthy marital situation. I didn't know how I was going to get through it, but god never left me and showed me himself time after time. He was my resource. I questioned myself and why I was in this mess for years. Or if I left the situation sooner would things be different.

What was all this for?

How am I benefiting from this?

Maybe I went through this to help someone else. I didn't need anyone to judge my situation. You won't understand it until you are in it or went through it. Too many questions ran through my mind. I was mentally tapped out. I was tired. I felt weary and I had so much doubt.

My insecurities were all over the place and it just wasn't fair. But my help comes from the lord and he heard my cry. With patience, prayer and developing an understanding, everything I lost in this journey was replaced in a special way. And I learned to find happiness in everyday things.

Sometimes our worst situations can bring out the best in us. It can push us to do more. If we let it. Its normal to feel overwhelmed and get discouraged. Trust me I had and still have plenty of those days. But it's easier to keep pushing and keep telling yourself you got this. You may have

moments when you feel like you failed. That's ok.
When we fail, we learn. When we learn, the wiser
we become.

That's when growth sets in.

WHEN YOU FEEL

ALONE, YOUR NOT.

GOD IS WITH YOU

EVERY STEP

OF THE WAY

When I was struggling with anxiety from domestic abuse I didn't drive. When I overcame anxiety I finally started driving, god blessed me to get a car, and my driving skills got better.

This was big for me and I am very proud of myself.

Our challenging situations can take you to places mentally that you would never think you would be. Nothing we go through is ever a waste ladies. It's what we take from that's important. If we go through something it may seem rough, and it seems like it won't pass, but there is always a purpose.

Sometimes it's hard to see the purpose. I had to pray and ask god for mine. I'm still trying to fully understand it now.

I have become a stronger person knowing that whatever challenge comes my way with god on my side I can get past it.

To heal from the domestic violence situation, I suddenly had the desire to visit women in domestic violence shelters and coordinate encouraging activities. These activities were therapeutic for me. It helped me to be around others who would totally understand my story and how I was feeling.

They have been through it. It also helped me to see how blessed I was to be alive and how to cope with my feelings. For a while I ignored my feelings and tried to push without really taking care of me. When I realized that healing takes time, I felt better about who I was. I accepted the fact that it was ok to have those moments. Its ok to feel lost at times and to cry. Its all a part of the healing process. The best part of the healing process is discovering who you really are.

I have learned there are four stages of healing. The first stage is grief and denial. Of course, we are all strong and some things are really hard to accept. Especially without blaming ourselves, thinking this can't be my life or what I have to deal with. For me this was the biggest part of the process.

"OUR PAST IS NOT

OUR FUTURE.

HOW WELL WE MOVE

FORWARD IS WHATS

IMPORTANT"

-CYNTHIA MARSHALL

I had to accept the loss of everything. The idea of starting over was a mountain I thought I couldn't even begin to climb. The second stage is anger. We may not realize it but we are hurting ourselves holding on to anger. What are we gaining being angry at that person? I had to ask god to help me not to be angry at what this person did to me. Or not to be angry at my situation at the time.

I changed my thought process and asked god to help me get through it instead of focusing on what was done to me. This eventually gave me a sense of closure and peace. I was able to move forward by watching god work things out for me and my children. The third stage is depression. This part can be the heaviest and the one that last the longest. Like I stated I was mentally tapped out. I felt exhausted and I began to withdraw. I felt a loss of myself worth. I didn't feel valued as a person.

But then I remembered I can help encourage someone else. I'm not afraid to let someone know I've been there and every time I felt like giving up or I was at my last straw god saved me every time. Depression comes and goes or it can set in for a long time. It can really take over your thought process. I had to really focus on the future and the bigger picture.

Instead of thinking about what I didn't have any more I started being content with that I did have. That was when the unexpected blessings came.

I had to express myself some kind of way. I began to write my feelings down everyday and that was actually therapeutic for me. The last stage is acceptance. We have to accept where we are in life. No matter where we are. We grow from this stage because we are facing what is really there.

We are not our struggle that we may see. How we tackle what we are facing and how we overcome is where we start to see our strength. And that's when the best is brought out of us. That is when we realize that we are much stronger than what we really thought. The good thing is we survived it.

This process we overcame can help someone else. I can finally say that I accept me for me and I accept everything through these stages. We can move forward and become stronger than before.

Our past is not our present or future. I am not afraid to help someone else get through this process.

You never know what someone next to you is going through. Sometimes just listening will help anyone get through their own trials. Your testimony can take someone's beliefs so far without you even realizing it.

"Be of good

courage, and he

shall strengthen

your heart,

all ye that hope

in the Lord".

Psalms 31:24 (KJV)

Focus on ways to love yourself. Take the time to get to know who you really are. I still practice this because its impossible for me to love myself if I barely know who I AM. Our journey helps us to get to know ourselves. And when we love ourselves we will be able to love others. I try to also focus on my strengths to help with having positive feelings about myself.

One of the self-love activities I do is writing down my accomplishments. Sometimes reminding yourself what you have accomplished will make and help you want to do more. I need to add to my accomplishment list. Setting goals, even daily goals is positive energy towards your day. Another activity that worked for me was writing a love letter to myself. This letter sounds easy, but it actually took time for me. It helped me to identify all the things I actually liked about myself.

Having a good cry is also good. Letting our emotions out is very important it's a way of expressing your feelings. Ive cried to myself many days and sometimes when you don't have the words to express, crying can really help with that.

This was a journey that god brought me through and he can do the same for you. I've learned so much about myself. And I'm still learning. There is always purpose in your pain and nothing once again is a waste. My process and journey helped me to see whats important and I hope yours helps you too. I love myself and I am finally happy with who I am today. With god I embrace my challenges because I know that he will bring me through it.

Every women has her own journey and we all should add to it in a positive way. It's our job to empower each other and it will help our journey. Let's motivate ourselves and others to be great, successful, and strong.

So, what else is important to me now? My happiness, peace of mind, stability, my two beautiful children, and most of all my relationship with god. When that is strong there is nothing else I will have to worry about. For it is god who constructed and empowered my journey.

I pray this helps bring a positive light to your journey. You are not alone and no matter what, in gods eyes your journey is special.

"HAVE HOPE,

HAVE FAITH,

AND

DON'T FORGET

OUR PAIN

TODAY WILL BE OUR

GREATEST

STRENGTH

TOMORROW"

-CYNTHIA MARSHALL

"For I know the plans I have for you, declares the lord, plans to prosper you and not to harm you, plans to give you hope and a future."

Jeremiah 29:11 (NIV)

CONSTRUCTING & EMPOWERING A WOMEN'S JOURNEY DAILY WORDS OF EMPOWERMENT - CYNTHIA MARSHALL

I AM STRONG

I AM SUCCESSFUL

I AM BEAUTIFUL

I AM GREAT

I AM LOVED

I DESERVE THE BEST

I HAVE PATIENCE

I AM NOT AFRAID OF MY JOURNEY

I AM BLESSED

I AM VICTORIOUS

I AM FREE

Name 10 positive things about yourself

1.

2.

3.

4.

5.

6.

7.

8.

9.

10.

Name 5 things you want to accomplish in your life journey

1.

2.

3.

4.

5.

Write a love letter to yourself...........

_____

_____

_____

_____

_____

_____

_____

_____

_____

_____

_____

_____

_____

·

Printed in the United States
By Bookmasters